SURVIVING WORDS

Cover by Christian Knudsen from GUANAHUATO series, 1993.
Typeset by The Muses in 11 pt. Palatino

Acknowledgments
Some of these poems have appeared in Matrix.

I would like to thank Kenneth Radu, Karen Haughian, Ken Norris, Ruth Taylor, Odette Dubé, Linda Leith and Sharon H. Nelson for their advice and their critical eyes. I would also like to thank the Canada Council and Ministère de la Culture for the financial aid that gave me the time to work on this book.

Published with the assistance of the Canada Council and Le Ministère de la Culture.

Printed and bound in Canada by Imprimerie d'éditions Marquis Ltée.

Dépôt légal, Bibliothèque Nationale du Québec
and the National Library of Canada, 4th trimester, 1994

Canadian Cataloguing in Publication Data

Farkas, Endre, 1948—
Surviving Words

Poems.
ISBN 0-919754-49-X

1. Political poetry, Canadian (English).
I. Title.

PS8561.A72S87 1994   C811'.54   C94-900516-9
PR9199.3.3F37S87 1994

The Muses' Company
P.O. Box 214
Ste. Anne de Bellevue
Québec, Canada
H9X 3R9

SURVIVING WORDS

ENDRE FARKAS

THE MUSES' COMPANY/LA COMPAGNIE DES MUSES

For Eva Weisz and Sándor Farkas, much more than survivors.

CONTENTS

HEIRLOOM

THE PROMISED LAND

IN THE MIDDLE OF THE NIGHT

HEIRLOOM

HEIRLOOM

for A.M. Klein

I was conceived by lovers bound for Auschwitz,
Belsen, Birkenau, Buchenwald, Mauthausen,
and every other camp that was,
is and ever will be.

I am the seed of every man-child
who was rounded up like livestock,
loaded into cattle-cars
and shipped off to a final solution.

I grew in the womb of every woman
who was shaved, tattooed
and lined up naked
next to gas chambers.

I am a child of children
stripped of their innocence in death camps;
torn from grief-numbed parents who knew
but were helpless and were gassed
and cremated into Pure Jews.

I am their next day
starved on stale bread
and crumbs of that
saved for tomorrow
in case things got worse.

I am their rememberance of home;
how right now,
this would be happening,
that would be talked about,
and Oh the food—
cooked,
served,
given thanks for,
eaten!

I am their luck, stumbled into;
an extra potato peel in the slop
grabbed quickly, gratefully,
without the strength to question.

I am their songs
begun by mad, angelic voices
which would not be silenced:
which grew wings and flew into their hearts,
and let them escape for a minute
the barbed wires, the towers,
the smokestacks and the soap.

I am their endless stories
retold between endless roll-calls,
between endless hard labour,
between endless beatings,
between endless deaths,
and a moment of sleep.

And through the telling
be safe, beautiful,
full of life.

I am their hope
(some called it God)
when none is possible
because they know no better
because they know nothing else *is* possible.

I am their noble lineage,
their proud ancestry.

I am their priceless heirloom
hidden from murderers
where it could not be found.

I am their surviving words.

WHAT HAPPENED: EVA'S STORY

I

What happened to youth?
What happened to that young girl in the photograph
standing in her father's yard
in her simple dressing gown
embracing a book
smiling?

Men in well-tailored, leather coats
pounded on my door,
broke into my life,
ripped it like a photograph
and shipped me to Auschwitz.

I stood naked
in the light of day
my life, a man's whim.

With a towel and a bar of soap,
I waited.

The need for slaves saved me;
returned me to the living.

WORK WILL MAKE YOU FREE.

They starved me,
worked me past exhaustion,
dared me to buckle;
to commit that deadly sin.

One day my twelve-year old sister
threw me her piece of stale bread
and I never saw her again.

II

What happened after?

Liberation
and the rest of my life.

Work,
from before light
to after dark,
stitching my life into every sleeve,
into every pocket, into every lining
of every piece I ever sewed.

The tattooing of sewing machines,
the explosions of buttonhole machines,
the suffocating steam of pressing machines
dulled the forever migraine of remembering.

III

What now?

Free from work,
I double lock my door,
stay up late,
read romances,
and remember
a photograph.

Behind the blinding white-light nausea
well-tailored men are pounding in my head.

I shut my eyes and shout
at a God I still believe in

What happened?

Reflection: Sándor's Story

In the camp
everyday was a lifetime.
Everyday I expected death;
was more certain of it than the daily, dry piece of bread.

And then,
from one day to the next,
I am free.

Freedom is
a man, unguarded,
unshaven, with sunken cheeks,
wandering and seeing
a man, unguarded,
unshaven, with sunken cheeks
staring back
perplexed.

He was skin on bones
drawn tight as a drum skin;
a stranger in pyjama pants too big,
holding them up by the drawstring.

I couldn't imagine who it was;
a stranger, another survivor
looking, desperate
for a familiar detail.

I shuffled up to him
and asked his name.
His cracked, hungry lips
asked me the same.

I argued with him.
He argued with me.

Then a shiver,
like the dead up a chimney,
slipped up my spine,

froze us
into breath-stopping silence.

MOTHERS' DAY: ANOTHER STORY

I

We were marched day and night.

We knew what was going on;
only the dead didn't.

My friend and I made a pact
at dusk, we would step out of line.

Hand squeezing hand,
waiting for the shots,
we held our breaths
and stepped into the night.

II

Removing our yellow stars,
we became shadows.

Morning brought us to a village,
the market-day crowd hid us.

We searched for a kind face
that would believe our story
of running from the Russians.

III

One kind soul took us in.
I gave her my good shoes.
A day later the police came.

All right you Dirty Jews
two days rest is enough for you!

I'm not Jewish
I wailed.
Just look at my face!
I'm a good Christian!
I swear I am!
I lied

Then recite the Lord's Prayer!

What did I know of the Lord's prayer?
I knew the Jew's blessing for bread.

Our Father
Who art in heaven,
my friend began,
Hallowed be Thy name
Thy kingdom come.
I mumbled along.
Thy will be done
on earth,
as it is in heaven.
Give us this day
our daily bread.
And forgive us our trespasses
as we forgive those
who trespass against us.
And lead us not into temptation
but deliver us from evil.

Amen!

All right. Go!

IV

With forged papers
making me a pure Christian,
I got a job in a shoe factory
and lived in a bombed-out place
until it was condemned and I was moved
to a building that turned out to be
a safe house for Jews.

Wallenberg Jews.
Rich Jews with Swedish papers
but starving,
forbidden out until 11:00 a.m.
By then all the bread, fruit,
meat and vegetables were gone.

So I volunteered.
Every early morning,
like a pack mule,
I hauled food from the market.

They never offered me any.

V

The major in charge had flour and yeast
and gave me some in return for baking him bread.
He loved my bread.

With my yeast and flour
I made bread for the Jews.

VI

The Russians arrived.
I toldthe Jews that I was a Jew.
They didn't believe me.
I looked too Christian.
They made me recite the blessing for bread.

> Blessed art Thou
> Our Lord our God
> King of the Universe
> who brings forth bread from the earth.

> Amen!

They never thanked me.

VII

I returned home.
My mother didn't.

WITNESSES REPORT

20,000 a day gassed.
Every week a city disappeared.

And when the killing didn't go fast enough
children were thrown into fires,

alive;
like potatoes.

No one smelled anything.
Nothing happened.

AUSCHWITZ

Auschwitz
was a huge SS-run security area
in Upper Silesia.

According to the latest calculations
1.1 million Jews
from all over Europe were sent there.
960,000 were murdered immediately.

In March 1941,
SS chief Heinrich Himmler
ordered that work start
on Auschwitz II.

Auschwitz was equipped with a mortuary
that in 1941
the SS converted into a gas chamber
and later turned into an air-raid shelter.

When the gas chambers and crematoria
were working full capacity,
as in the summer of 1944,
more than 20,000 people a day were annihilated.

When Soviet troops liberated Auschwitz
they found 840,000 items of women's clothing,
43,525 pairs of shoes, 460 artificial limbs,
and seven tonnes of human hair.

In 1947,
the Polish government decreed
Auschwitz a state museum.

In 1948,
it was decided to reconstruct
the gas chamber and the ovens.
Today
no one is certain
whether the vents for inserting the poison gas
are exactly where they were originally located.

Effective conservation did not take place until the late 1950s
by which time terrible damage had been done.
It was not until 1962 that a protection zone
was created around the main sites.

Nine years later
Auschwitz was added by UNESCO
to the World Heritage List.

Experts from around the world
were recently invited to examine
the Auschwitz problem
and pool ideas for its preservation.

Authorities pledged to maintain
the original character of the place.

They face a huge and disturbing task.

Facts from "The Auschwitz Question"
by David Cesarini.

LIBERATION IS

one morning
without guards

silence
in a concentration camp

a Black American sergeant
machine-gunning the gates

waves of Russian tanks
rolling over barbed wire

years of tears flowing
uncontrollably

the emaciated storming the food depot
gorging to death on fistfuls of lard

waking from a coma

greeting yourself in a mirror
as you would a stranger

being told to go home

avoiding rape
by telling liberating soldiers
that you've got "the disease"

walking down familiar roads
stopping at familiar houses
knocking on familiar doors
to see who returned

finding out what parts of you are missing

arriving home

staring at old neighbours
staring from windows and doorways
watching your return

a different silence

NOTHING

I

Nothing is forgotten.
Nothing is ever forgotten.
Everything becomes a memory hummed;
a lullaby for babes suckling at breasts.
Everything becomes a myth
passed on by the old sitting on benches at sunset.

My father remembers
childhood best friends
playing in each others' yards,
sharing hunger in each others' kitchens.

He remembers World War II
coming to his village
and those childhood best friends
playing hide and seek for real,
becoming part of the mob
that cheered the round-up.

He remembers returning
to warm greetings by old pals
who were truly glad to see him
and wanted to begin again from scratch.

He forgot.
Nothing happened.

II

He learned in '56,
when the glorious revolution
stampeded our village,
time neither heals
nor forgets.

The battle cry was
        The blood of Commies
        and those Dirty Jews.

His old pals were familiar by their nightly howling,
their footsteps on cobblestone roads.

For him, it was frightening echo;
for me, an unexpected inheritance.

III

In '94 on TV,
neighbours in old Yugoslavia
sitting on benches at sunset
talk of how their lives,
Serb and Bosnian,
are intertwined;
how they shared everything before
and will forever.

They swear
it won't happen there.

But the war,
as it does,
as it must,
spreads its poison
and soon:
they do not visit,
do not sit together
do not talk *to* each other
but *about*.

They tell stories to themselves
about what they've always suspected—
there really is a difference
and recall ancient tribal grudges.

The radio plays the old songs
of the good-old days.
Feelings thought long gone
are remembered again.

Nothing is forgotten.

IV

My father remembers his visit
to the town he was born in '21,
to the town he was deported from in '44,
to the town he had to flee in '56.

Back to visit his parents' graves,
to remember.

Returning from the cemetary
to the house he used to live in,
he found old friends sitting stiff and formal
but before they had a chance to rise
he asked
      Friends,
      where were you when I needed you?

He could not,
would not let them forget again.

They filed out in a silence they will long remember.

V

Betrayal is always and everywhere,
passed on like an heirloom.

The show ends, always,
with neighbour shooting neighbour
right through the heart.

WHY IS THIS NIGHT DIFFERENT FROM ANY OTHER?
Passover, March 26, 1994

And it came to pass.

Survivors,
the children of survivors
and their children gather
at the table set with bitter
and sweet testaments
to hardships and triumphs.

In the formal unease of exiles,
we, the children of survivors
who have wandered far from home,
have left behind more than countries of birth
and mother tongues,
return as strangers among strangers,
guests without a home,
even at home.

Only survivors believe.

Children of survivors
grown busy with their lives
half-listen to sounds of their ancient tongue,
the murmured prayers of thanksgiving,
and go through the motions.

The first-born son asks the questions
tripping over words in a way
that his children find funny.

Between tears that choke like gas,
the survivor remembers his Egypt.

It was exactly fifty years ago tonight
they broke into our poor homes,
into our poor lives.

There was no blood on our doors
to protect us from this plague.

Thousands of us were rounded up,
deported by a few with machine guns.

They were the law.
We were the criminals.

They made us believe it.

Words can never say enough
or make you feel our helplessness.

We were marched through
each day of nothingness.

Starving, we shuffled
into nothingness.

Every night
they would fire into the crowd.

And next morning
the living would continue.

There was no miracle,
no closing of the sea over these Egyptians.

Who could have imagined what they had in mind?
Not even five thousand years of stories.

And even after all this, I still believe.

How,
looking at the children,
can I not?

FOR THOSE WHO DENY THE HOLOCAUST

I

Okay
there weren't six million killed.

For you
a special. . .five and a half.

FOR THOSE WHO DENY THE HOLOCAUST

II

May you wake one fine morning
and outside your window,
in a tree hear the birdies sing

WORK WILL MAKE YOU FREE

May you rise from your comfortable bed
and rub your bloated belly
and scratch your empty head
and step into the shower

and then, for a moment,
as you're about to run the water
may you doubt
the religion of your plumber.

For Those Who Deny The Holocaust

III

You have such a fine Aryan body
and so much of it.

Imagine what could be done with it:
the fat boiled down to make pure Aryan soap
and that pure Aryan skin,
tanned and stretched. . . .

There'd be enough for a lampshade or two
and lots left over for scrolls
on which to inscribe the names of the dead
who were never exterminated.

FATHERS & SONS

Before the New Year's first meal,
the ritual as prescribed by ancient laws,
the benediction.

Your finger tips
form a temple roof over me,
your eyes close, lips murmur a prayer
calling upon God to bless your child.

Quiet tears follow, flow
down the riverbeds of your cheeks.

They bless. They plead.
I taste them.

I am the prodigal son;
a false messiah
who haunts your dreams and desires
and returns each New Year
to be locked in your loving embrace.

Exiled from each other by our lives,
we live in foreign lands.

We do not speak of flight
but say all is well, all is right.

Tonight my son scurries to my bed
for an embrace against the night.

I hold him tight and comfort
even though I know
all sons are lost
even when they return
and all fathers fail
even when they bless.

JEWS

They are The Chosen:
the ones who signed The Covenant,
delivered The Word
and constantly argue with God.

They are The Wanderers
who honour learning
because it is holy
and easy to pack at a prophet's notice.

They are Christ-killers,
bloodthirsty and dirty,
which excuses everything done to them
for millennia by the millions.

They are Shylocks,
international conspirators,
accountants, bankers, wholesalers,
jewing the world for their pound of flesh.

But now we know them better.
They are also cruel, ignorant
dealers in death; not so special
no more chosen than others.

They, too, use terror and torture
and have their own secret police
to guard with deadly weapons
their camps of barbed wire fences.

They are like everyone else
with their own land to protect,
who prefer the Golan Heights for their big guns sites
to the moral high ground and their ancient rites.

They have lost the victims' edge,
have become what they always were:
a people who follow visions and orders
and must be held accountable for that.

DREAM

With dreams upon my bed thou scarest me
& affrightest me with visions

William Blake

It is daytime and the sun is shining.
I'm walking down a city street.
Could be in any city
but I sense more than know
that it's my city's street:
the textures, angles and smells
make it mine.

I am with my wife
in a crowd,
when out of nowhere,
smiling skinheads,
like they were the law,
encircle us.

With averted eyes
the world strolls by.

The skins swarm,
brush, bump;
become a tightening noose.

I am crying
trying to yell
this is not real,
there is no sense to this!

The churning bile,
the fist-tight clenched jaw,
the waves of nausea,
the helplessness
overwhelms.

      No, not again.
I cry in defeat.

      No, not again!
I howl

and attack and break free,
run around a corner
stop, turn and see

my wife,
laughing,
joining in the chase.

CROSSING

The first step forward
is into No-man's land,
where by mutual consent,
nothing is allowed to grow,
where anything moving
is suspect and fair game
for the border guards.

O moonless night, come!
We give ourselves up to you;
pray, love us enough
to hide us, to shield us,
to guide us.

We leave everything behind
except a clean change of underwear
and a few dollars hidden in them.

We find ourselves lost
in the desert of mud;
wandering exiles,
only ourselves as guides,
seeking the other side,
the promised land.

We sink into deceptively deep ditches,
claw our way up gravel embankments,
find lost children crying in the wilderness,
abandon hope and
by some miracle
arrive on the other side.

After No-man's land comes the ocean
a deeper darkness to cross.

We lie on our rolling bunks
and vomit up everything,
even what we don't have.
For days we empty
into the endless, depthless ocean.

We vomit neighbours
and friends who betrayed us.

We feel the desire to die
and lie on our bunks practicing.

And just when we think our prayers
are about to be answered,
there is news of land:
the New World.

We touch its shore,
the nausea ceases
almost instantly.

We are embraced by winter.
Its icy wind stings us to tears,
its long cold kisses sink into every pore.

At least,
it's a welcome
and that's a welcome change.

In our green language
we call this white land home.

You Know

I

You know
every immigrant is a story.

You know;
the stranger in a strange land.

You know
so much depends on knowing
what you don't.

II

Leaving her hostile homeland
crossing No-man's land,
and sea-sick distances
she arrives.

Free
and desperate to say something,
she is a mute on the back balcony of a new country;
a *greener* facing a new neighbour
who knows that she doesn't know
the language,
so,
out of kindness,
speaks louder.

My mother watches her mouth move:
rapid, mysterious sounds
explode from her face.

Almost, sometimes,
she can make out shadows of words
	You know?
	You know?

punctuates the neighbour's babble.

	No
is a word an immigrant learns quickly
even before the curses.
Listening to her neighbour's constant
	you know
gets to her.

She shouts back
	I No! I No! I No!
until it sounds like the hurling of pots and pans.

III

You know
she's nothing if not determined:
a survivor of the grammarians of extermination.

So
night after night;
after sweatshop hours,
she sits in immigrant classes
with other awkward mouths
twisting their lips to master the new words,
new worlds that would make her feel at home.

	Hello.
	How are you?
	Fine thank you.
	And you?
	I am fine thank you.

44

She gags on chalk placed under the tongue
to get those *th* sounds of
    the and *think*
    and *thank you*
to slip out smoothly as her breath.

Her twisted tongue works hard
and cries and curses.

She learns to conjugate.
She watches the future become the past too fast.

She curses the language of this place
but curses more the language of the old country;
a language of beautiful poetry and pure hate.

IV

Often, late at night in the quiet light,
in the white light of memory,
she sits in her dressing gown
and reads.

She takes pride in her comprehension
and in her simple phrases
that, to her, seem seamless
as the clothes she's sewn for over thirty years.

Though she will never fully chart this language
she can say,
almost perfectly,

    This language is my land now.
    You know?

THE PROMISED LAND

The Promised Land

I

I return.

The bile
of exile coats my tongue.

Revenge is mine,
is in my art.

The guilt
of being the victim unnerves me.

II

Naked,
without time to be innocent.

Against the world.
Naked.

Do you remember?

It's an old story; old as stories,
always new to someone.

I remember.

It is '56.

Somewhere the dream is good.
Somewhere the revolution is good.

Here,
marauding along the cobbled village streets:
the nightmare,
the lynch mob of the night thumps against the gates.

Ours is barnwood gray
and bolted
contains a home, a well,
and our neighbours
the blacksmiths.

These men, who fire up the morning,
who show us how to work and play with fire,
become our guardians, our sun;
decent, nothing more than human
while others become less;
what we must fear, and
rage, burn, beat and pillage
under the safe hood of night.

III

The mask is the times
The mask is the mob.
The mask is the excuse.
The mask is the torch.
The mask again.

IV

In the morning
everyone goes to market
praising the revolution
smiling, nodding

as if to say
nothing happened.

Nothing happened.

My mother,
hand in pocket
wrapped around the kitchen knife,
nods back silently
and vows

Never Again!

Nothing happened.

V

In school
I am called to the front;
called as if to recite a poem,
a lullaby whose lines still haunt me,

and find myself encircled
and with the teacher's blessing
called names:
names as old as hate.

Nothing happened.

VI

My father,
remembers,
listens for old songs,
with a marching beat;
popular at such times in cafés and beer gardens
and makes plans to leave.

Oh how dangerous the empty synagogue,
the ancient rabbi, and the few surviving
Jews must be.

VII

I return in '91.

My hosts reassure me
most adamantly
those times when
nothing happened
are gone.

I am a comforted tourist in the country of my birth.

I visit an ancient synagogue,
marvel at the Mosque and Cathedral influences,
admire the arabesque decorations on its arches & domes,
stare at the packed-to-the rafters, non-existent Jews
murmuring prayers to their God
and sharing rumors of a bomb.

VIII

I return.

I am a child.
I am awake,
past my bed time,
far from home,
on the run.

I'm on the longest train ride of my life;
a train packed with others like us
whose mothers and fathers
sleep and travel light.

The conductor renames the train
the *Freedom Express*.
At each stop more get on.

At one
no one gets on
except the law in well-tailored leather coats.

The old order doesn't want us
to leave. They need us to hate us.

They take my mother's passport
and order us off.

Staying one step behind the law,
my father, in his leather coat,
becomes one of them,
pretends to be important,
shoves us into the washroom
and stands guard until we arrive at the end of the line.

IX

I am awake.
I am a child who will never sleep
the innocent sleep.

In a house in the woods
at midnight
we huddle.

A black-shawled old woman
sits in a corner staring at us, praying,
constantly crossing herself
like over the dead.

At midnight
the guide takes all our money,
tells us to go outside,
lines us up against the wall,
tells us to be silent,
tells us to wait and disappears
into the moonless night.

He calls out,
points into the total black
says
    go toward the light
says
    good-bye

says
    good luck.

X

At the edge here
the child says
        let's all hold hands and slide down.

And we all slide down
into the dark,
into the mud furrows seeded with mines

into No-man's land.

Here there is no direction.
Here/there in circles.
In circles, in circles,
in circles. . . .

Here is nowhere.
Here we hold hands.
Here we know the must of silence.

In circles
we struggle against the sucking mud,
searching for the straight line,
ducking the searchlights,
arriving where we do not know.

XI

We are always new to the place.
We are always in danger.
All ways.
Always looking out for signs,
songs, lines,
faces of memory

as old as memory.

I remember.

XII

It is '94.
        No end
And each night
            No end
in new confusion
                No end
all stops are illusions
                    No end
we have no choice
                    No end
we set out
                    No end

It is a time of chaos and unravelling
                        No end

Naming
Unnaming
                            No end

There is a revolution here
                            No end

I am back
in the promised land.

BUDAPEST BLUES

The dust of sadness fills the pores of Budapest
and the inbred, Hapsburg-pale, yellow walls
are stained forever by the acid tears of five-year plans.

At the bus stop, lung-choking dusk settles
on bent bodies weighted by years of waiting
for buses always packed and always late.

In their new freedom they huddle and pretend
that they do not see the Skinheads
beating up an old, Gypsy for a new Hungary.

I am watching this with a frightened eye.
I am glad that I am not from here.

But if not me, then who?
And if not now, when?

That's the Blues.

In Szeged Square[1]

O Hungary
lost in a familiar way
like one who was born here,
once lived here
but now is only a tourist
a long way from home,
I stop to watch
in Szeged Square
a young duo,
violin and flute
charm with Vivaldi
the old out of aging
the lovers into loving
but no one out of their money.

I watch three men
in faded-blue overalls
gather, deliberate, gesticulate
and finally,
with dull, primitive tools,
begin to chisel at a past
toward a future.

After an hour or so,
interrupted by leisurely expressos,
cigarette breaks and more debate,
they had neither broken through
nor repaired anything.

All around them
under socialist arches
under social-realist monuments
in Szeged Square
tomorrow begins now.

A flock of nervous, young, thin men
in expensive leather jackets hustle,
chatter, exchange money for money.

Anxious and willing
quick as a wink,
now that it's free,
they are ready,
to sell this passionate country.

[1]Szeged (seged) is a city in Southern Hungary on the Tisza River.

58

Morning in Szeged

Reluctantly
the sun opens its dying eye
on a dying world.

Below
like forgotten desires
shapeless figures stand
attached to lunch-filled briefcases.

A tired streetcar wobbles into sight
and with screeches of steel on steel
grinds to a halt.

Its spastic doors slam open,
swallow all
and like a stoic with heartburn
grimaces on.

In A Budapest Underpass

Old women who should be on porches,
gossiping about the passing world,
must again stand on worn-out feet
and sweet-sell crumbs: used shoes,
scraggly flowers and stained doilies
to pay for their death-wait
and hole in the ground.

Old men, scarecrow crucifixes,
who once proudly bartered long and hard,
sealed deals with a spit and a handshake,
now are eager to sell at any price:
old pants, old jackets, old raincoats
draped over outstretched arms,
and thank you for them

Men and women,
their future between shifts and lost jobs,
offer bags of darned socks,
lingerie once romantic;
anything and everything they can do without.

The children run around
call to and grab at passers by,
are busy buying and selling
sneakers, jeans, pornography
bullets and grenades.

Up against the wall
tired beyond tired,
they are the graffiti of the times:
the echoes of dead souls.

THE MISSING LINK

Ladies and gentlemen. Welcome and good evening.
We are here to announce an exciting new discovery.
We are here to unveil our find; to shed new light on
the missing link.

Voilà! The Neo-Nazi Man.

First observe his head: shaven,
hot waxed and immaculately polished.
Leading archeologists have said
that they have not seen the likes of it in years.

They say it resembles a penis with ears.

The bumps and ridges indicate,
to all the phrenologists,
amazing intelligence;
not a whit less than a picket fence.

Note the eyes; those hollow tiny holes,
keen as those of a little mole's.
They are so true, so Aryan blue,
and come alive at the sight of a Black, a queer or a Jew.

In public, he is shy.
Often his delicate face is masked by a bandanna
which he believes protects him, his soul,
from his predator, the international conspiracy,
that would steal his innocent, white beauty.

He walks upright just like the rest of us
leaving his hands free for grasping,
for making tools and fists.

He dresses in the latest combat gear
but claims there isn't any need to fear
because, he says,
he is here to do good deeds
like those folks in hoods and white sheets.

His favourite footwear is army boots
of the finest leather, with which he pledges
to make the world a better place.
The tough soles and steel toes
recall his ancestors,
the mighty men of goose-stepping rows.

A nocturnal creature,
he hunts in packs
dangerous tombstones
and new immigrants.

He has secret rituals and rites
and with fanatical devotion
prays to his god Genocide.

Around bonfires he tells stories;
tales of bravery, sacrifice,
scapegoats and glory.

He is a master of following orders.
His Sieg Heils,
a sign of his advanced philosophy,
reveal the depth of his sensitivity.

His leaders, also shy of light, teach
that all problems of racial pollution
have a clean and final solution.

The Neo-Nazi Man
claims superior genes
that place him above the rest;
makes him the Uberman
in his mythology.

To some he appears to be
no more than a minor irritation,
simple as a pimple,
but to others he is a messiah,
most welcome.

Beware.

The Neo-Nazi Man,
this missing link,
is the Phoenix
rising from the ashes of the night.

His brilliant shadow is a furnace
that devours all living light.

Night Life In Amsterdam

I

Everybody's got to eat
she said.

Ushered across an Italian-marble floor
I am seated in a Victorian, plush-red chair
of the rich, oak-paneled Vermeer Restaurant.

The tuxedoed Maitre d',
so handsome and elegant,
lights my candle
and recommends

a raw oyster on a half shell
with just a twist of lime
to prepare the palate

for the delicate cream of salsify soup
with translucent slices of truffle
floating, like unfurled water-lilies:

followed by the main course
of succulent grilled trout
surrounded by sweet baby carrots
and delicate slices of eggplant
sautéed in fresh butter.

And, of course, with it,
the perfect white wine:
Pouilly-Fuissé '86.

And for desert
a light, wonderful,
lemon-meringue mousse;
sweet with just a felicitous tang.

And, to finish,
cappuccino with a fine, dark, Dutch
chocolate-square floating on top.

And to satisfy the soul
Remy Martin.

He is right.

The food and the service
are excellent.

I cannot help but over-tip,
especially since it can be written off.

II

Business is business
she said.

The after-supper stroll in old Amsterdam
is the perfect constitutional.

Like the undulation of seductive hips,
the charming narrow, side streets lure me.

Into the night, into its history I flow and follow
to a street of windows filled with women
for rent.

A world of choice;
a menu of myriad shapes and colours,
fresh flesh from around the world,
under red lights every earthly delight
in delicious poses to satisfy
every man's every hunger.

And its government inspected.
What could be more civilized?

And it can be written off.

III

English? Français? Deutsch? Italiano?
she purrs.

Cat-like, before I know it,
in a luminescent, vinyl-green coat,
just a hint of pussy
meeting thigh-high vinyl black boots,
she is rubbing up against me.

She offers to do to me
what no one ever has
in a way no one ever will
for a price that can't be beat
and satisfaction guaranteed.

A true capitalist:
an independent

66

who hustles at her own speed,
keeps her own hours,
undercuts the state competition
but makes it up in volume.

She knows her business.

No is not an answer.
She offers a quick, free feel,
and just for me
a special special.

Like a knowing Maitre d'
sensing a difficult palate,
she suggests other delicious dishes;
girlfriends whose talents
she praises past the heavens.

Then her boyfriend
who is young and clean and,
her lips kissing her finger tips
declares a very tasty delicacy.

She wastes no more time
and instead of a good-bye
she says,
time is money
and money you need to eat.

And that
you can't write off.

LULLABY

The frightened heart
wakes with a start
and cries into the darkness

We are dying!

Oh hush my darling
don't you cry.
Oh hush my darling
and I will sing you a lullaby.

Oh yes my darling
we are dying,
sighing;
lying in each other's arms.

Oh yes my darling
we are dying,
forgetting;
fading with the music of our lives.

Oh my darling
we are dying,
lying;
buying each other in desperate bars.

Oh yes my darling
we are dying,
smiling;
having a hell of a good time.

Oh yes my darling
we are dying,
bleeding;
drowning in our raging blood.

Oh yes my darling
we are dying,
slipping;
sinking into No-man's mud.

Oh my darling
I wish I may and
I wish I might. . . .

Oh yes my darling
we are dying;
every night
we dream of this.

Oh hush my darling
we are dying.
Oh my darling
yes we are.

Oh my darling
the frightened heart
wakes with a start
cries into the darkness

    We are dying

and then falls back
to angelic sleep.

Oh hush my darling
don't you cry.

Oh hush my darling
and I will sing you a lullaby.

The Voyageurs
upon looking at Jean Steibruch's 1802 birchbark journal

From the tip of the island,
where geography and history merge
like streams into a mighty river;
flowing to God knows where,
men set out toward dreams of wealth
and canoe themselves into heroic tales.

To the rhythm of brave songs,
sad songs of leaving, songs of good company,
their aching arms paddle; go past fatigue,
to where their masters planned:
where each campsite and every meal
is religiously recorded.

Never knowing what comes next,
they ride turbulent rivers,
soak in frigid waters
and rename them
after saints and investors.

Canoes overhead and their trade on aching backs,
they portage raging rapids;
climb pathless hills, follow guides through forests
for the promise of fortunes ahead.

For the secrets of the land,
for native women,
for their winter warmth,
they learned ancient tongues
and left behind, pots, beads,
liquor, children and disease.

Tonight,
pounded by the howling winter wind,
blinded by swirling snow,
semis sneak past weigh stations,
zoom along the Transcanadian.

All along the road
the drivers talk to each other in manly code,
warn each other about the law,
pop pills to stay awake past sleep
and listen to the radio sing brave songs,
sad songs of leaving, and songs of good company.

This land is a lonesome highway
with long hours and heavy loads
hauled faster and further
than the law allows.

At truck stops, they fill up,
smoke and joke, and tell tall tales
about their lives to friendly waitresses
and to each other before
they pay and roll on.

They swear that their fortunes
are on this road, just over there,
just around the next bend,
just after the next load.

This is their land, their history,
their myth; still in the making.
Aching shoulders and bent backs
still dream,
and day and night still haul
for the company of wealthy men.

VAUDREUIL BAY

after Bruegel's *Les Chasseurs dans la neige*

A snap-crack-your breath
brilliant and blinding,
January blue-sky day
canopies the evergreen-embraced,
frozen-over Vaudreuil Bay.

In phosphorescent-orange, red and
silver overalls, fishermen sit
on upturned plastic-bright, white buckets
watching over lines for a tug of life
and with land-of-plenty ease
hook and pluck fish onto the shimmering ice.

Leaping for liquid air,
they wriggle and flip
like ice-capade clowns,
land with a thwack,
and lie there drowning.

Children on Christmas skates wobble;
hold on to each other for dear life.

Their whoops of joy and squeals of fear
slide across the frozen bay.

They glide in circle games
about the kind, smiling men
staring at the wide-eyed fish.

And for an instant
they know something.

And then
skate on.

THE HUNTERS
for Raymond Souster

The blasts of horns
loud and long
followed by staccato bursts
announce their coming.

Curtains part.
Women in polyester housecoats,
and Phentex slippers, spill out
into the bone-cold November light,
line the sidewalk,
jump up and down,
wave and shout.

The victors are home;
fists in clenched salute
they point to the spoils
spread eagled on the tops of their vans.

The men bounce out,
swagger, await the rush
and embrace of their women.
They are as they imagined.

The women get cameras, wine and beer.
The men climb up to their kills.

One grabs the antlers like a rodeo steer wrestler.
One kneels and puts his arm around its neck like a dear pal.
One puts its head on his lap like a favourite dog.

They are heroes.

And they know
there's going to be
heavy fucking tonight.

DORION SUITE

PRELUDE

The night is a nocturnal mouth
devouring what it can;
what it must and then
full of itself, sighs
and falls asleep.

I

Mourning doves,
sensual breaths,
greet the morning
with a bluesy duet.
Always in pairs,
they tango through the dew
pecking the grass for grub.

The blue jay,
the one with the limp,
eyes the kitchen from her perch for signs of life,
spots it and begins her ritual begging
extending her lame leg for pity.

She swoops and scoops the peanuts
with military precision.

She guards her domain ruthlessly.
Ask the wounded grackle
who buries his head in his bruised wing,
caws, from his safe, fence-post distance,
a stay-away song but only until hunger
begins to gnaw again.

The squirrels are skittish:
cautious two-steps follow quick hops,
at-attention sudden stops,
and off-again-darts
to collect whatever they can.

The cat lies flat-cat-still,

stares
    slithers
            pounces.

More often than not
misses.

But there are days. . . .

II

Crocuses,
their green ears close to the ground
and saffron eyes open for unseasonable surprises,
send back news of Spring
and soon others follow.

Narcissus,
bundled in their winter bulbs,
are holed up underground.
But even in sleep the grizzly veterans
are always on alert for those first signs
that signal the Spring offensive.

They slither through the rich decay of corpses,
up through the crumbling crust and charge
to become the colours of life.

A myriad of shapes and smells
invade the garden and infiltrate the air.

We grow them for their beauty,
fragrance and seductiveness:
cut them to traffic in love.

But it's not for us
they flaunt their colours or spice,
not for our desires they open their petals wide.

Like us,
they'll do what they must to survive.

To everything there is a reason.

III

And what do we make
of these strange appendages
growing out of us
suggesting intimate relationships
with doves, jays, grackles,
squirrels, cats and plants?

What of the imagination
that makes a poem of devouring,
sees life as the self-serve Universal Restaurant
with everyone on the menu?

Why compose symphonies out of chatter
to grace our daily gestures?

Why flesh out shapes and sounds
and sing love songs?

IV

Across the street
a woman wears clothes too-tight
and sits on her front steps
composing a poem of unrequited love.
She hungers for a rhyme.

The stripper on the balcony
peels men till only she is left
sunning, howling country tunes
about being lonely.

Next door the young mother;
almost single,
with a biker's tongue,
joins her
and they sing their way
through these fucking, hard, hungry times.

V

The evening draws the blinds.
The starving night comes with its open mouth.

Another hunger
eats away at us

night and day.

In The Middle Of The Night

IN THE MIDDLE OF THE NIGHT
for E. L-R.

In the middle of the night,
when ominous knocks
frighten half the world,
a friend calls.

His words touch
the way the blind see,
caress, squeeze and leave fingerprints
on horrors we dare not name.

Tortured and called a fool
by brave men with electric courage
who, with families to feed,
did their best not to be next.

He confessed to silence practiced in screams.
He learned to forget numbers, names, friends.
He learned how to dress well for the revolution.

In the middle of the night,
when all over the world
mass graves are filled
with *the disappeared*,
a friend calls.

He says he forgives.
He longs to say hello.

CONFESSION

Don't call me an animal.
I am a man, just like you.

I give them every chance I can.
I start by sweet talking them,
offer cigarettes, promise fair treatment;
even release.

And if they insist on ignorance or principles,
I try to convince them its futile;
that in the greater scheme of things,
it is trivial.

Why resist?
In the end we'll all be worm food.
Until then might as well eat well,
sleep in unlocked rooms, unafraid of midnight steps.
No ideal survives man's ingenuity for pain.
Trust me.

I have a family and many mouths to fill.
Look here is a picture of my wife and children.
I've got a heart, just like you.

I just follow orders.
And if I don't do it, someone else will.
Under the right conditions
so would you.

And that's the honest truth.

Now A Word From Our Sponsor

You've tried Massacres, Slavery,
The Inquisition, Witch Hunts,
Genocide, Apartheid, Holocaust
Final Solution
and a host of others.

But they all left you dissatisfied.

But Now!
Brand New!
Improved!

Ethnic Cleansing!

Developed by the best minds,
using the latest technology.

Ethnic Cleansing!

A detergent so effective
you will not believe your eyes.

Ethnic Cleansing!

So powerful that
it will remove all stains.

Ethnic Cleansing!

Will make everything
cleaner than clean,
purer than pure!

Ethnic Cleansing!

With its secret ingredients,
ancient as mankind,
will make you feel good
all over!

Ethnic Cleansing!

So good
you'll think
you're back in the good old days!

And best of all,

Ethic Cleansing

leaves no trace!
leaves no after smell!

Ethnic Cleansing!

It works!

Try it!
You'll like it.

Ethnic Cleansing!

LETTER FROM NICARAGUA

My mother is a very humble lady
but very kind.

My grandmother doesn't live with us
but she loves me.

My mother helps her in the home
to sew people's clothes.

My community is Nueva Libia.
Its inhabitants are very humble
but work together to achieve their goal.

Write me
and tell me about the natural beauties
of your country.

Hiroshima Haiku

A baby wakes up.
The mother goes to comfort.
It is August 6th.

WISDOM OF THE EAST
for M.K.

Ancient wisdom says

in time of hunger
discard heavy load.

A she-child,
a burden of poverty;
worthless property,
takes up too much room
at an already overcrowded table.

Barefoot,
barely able to toddle,
she still needs a finger to clasp.

Abandoned.
In the winter mountains,
the cold, brilliant sun watches.

Ancient wisdom says

luck twists and turns
like mountain paths:
good follows bad.

It leads her to here,
to making heavenly angels in the Canadian snow.

After sipping hot cocoa, she says
she knows how to say
in her abandoned language

> *Mommy,*
> *Daddy,*
> *I'm hungry.*

In The Heat Of The Night

Last night we made love.
We crossed borders
and traveled countries without fear.
With bouquets of kisses
we welcomed each other as heroes
who had conquered no one.
Implosions of ecstasy everywhere
and we breathed as one.
Unafraid, naked,
curled into each other,
we slept and dreamed.

Tonight to war.
Men and their machines are on the move.
Tanks roll in, roll over the gritty flesh of sand.
Snipers take aim,
fingers stroke well oiled triggers.
And tonight's ecstasy
is within hairline sights.

Killing is best done at night
when the senses are most keen
and imagination most vivid
in conjuring up terror in the shadows
cast by the lyric moon.

Howling humans, predators
are sinking their manufactured talons
into their own kind.

Love, the morning-light reveals
shrapnel-gouged holes in faces,
spurting blood and
evaporating steam-of-life
from where the belly was.

The brilliant sun
rises
from the burnt out eyes of the dead.

WINTER STORM

Winter winds swirl up a storm,
frighten the night awake;
howl like sirens in the Middle East
thousands of miles from here.

The howling siren song,
wails against wall and windows,
like mourners over corpses
and interrupts the film
War And Peace.

It is bitterly cold.
I switch off the TV.
I have read the book.
I know how it ends.

I write down my fears:
helpless, helpless, helpless.

I know children are crying,
dying.

I look in on mine,
give thanks
and turn out the lights.

The howling wind.
The raging storm.

O GOD

Hi.
This is God.
I'm not home right now and won't be for a while
but if you care to leave a message after the deluge
I may get back to you later.

O God
I know you're busy.
What with your hot-lines lighting up day and night:
the flood of calls from Popes, Ayatollahs,
Rabbis and Evangelists,
all claiming to be old friends from way back when,
calling, wanting a sign to show the masses
to keep them coming back for more.
And important world leaders,
all asking for a blessing for their nation
and their important killing dreams,
and from lesser known dictators of fourth-rate powers
who want just a small nod for a tiny, local massacre,
genocide, ethnic cleansing or clan revenge and of course
each of us waiting to get through.
Well. . .I understand why you got an answering machine.

Actually I don't want anything.
Just called to say Hi
and let you know I'm also on a sabbatical.
And I figured,
since we haven't talked in a while
we could get together at some quiet café
over cappuccino or a beer
and discuss IT,
or talk about the idea of original sin
or maybe shoot a game of pool.

You could tell me what sign you are
or if you're seeing anyone
or exchange a few jokes
(you've probably heard them all)
or tell me about what's love got to do with IT?

Or whatever else comes to mind.

I've been thinking about you;
and just want to let you know
that you're a damn good concept
but hell in the hands of those
who'd make a temple of you:
must be our desire for order
and fear of loneliness.

Are you responsible for IT?

But what if you don't exist and I'm just imagining this;
making up this stuff about your answering machine.

I feel as if I've just gotten hold of an enigma by the horns.

Oh what a difference it would make
to know for certain
whether you do or don't exist.
I guess you know
we have this desperate need to know.

Is curiosity a gift or a curse?
Did you give it to us on purpose?

Do you answer to a higher being?
Are you just following orders?

I'm no theologian
just someone with time on his hands
listening to the buzz in his head;
staring at the empty page,
scared of it.

Were you ever scared, unsure?
In the beginning?
Are we the words you fill your pages with?

You sure do bring out the serious in us.

I said I didn't want anything,
just to hang out if you felt like it
but I guess you can see through me.

Anyway
I thought I'd give you a shout
and see if you were free.
So if you are, give me a call.

And if I'm not in
leave a message on the machine
and I'll get back to you as soon as I can.

Bye.

NOTES IN NEW YORK BLUE
                    for M.G.

La Guardia.
In the traffic of people ascending and descending,
we are greeted by chanting worshippers in saffron robes,
and polite young men and women
selling flowers in the name of the moon.

On the traffic jammed road to the Big Apple
young hoods in leather jackets
walk along the dividing lines
hustling hot, car phones.

The Port Authority.
Buses from all over the world pull in;
their fumes tanning the city's skin.

We walk between them
eyes averted from sad men
drinking out of paper bags.

A curse and a bottle flies by our heads.
They are the instruments and music of the city.

There are wreathes of glistening razor wires
crowning fences and roof tops
of important buildings.

There is a need, there is a reason.

On the street Americans have
fine-tuned the American dream
into a scam.

What used to be a young man
comes to us crying for a bed to die in.

We all want it to be over.
In homes, a sadness under the skin
has slipped in despite the dead bolts.

There are no curtains just bars of fear and loneliness.
Behind each, hope is shot into veins.

We sit in front of the screen
watching a man scream

      This gun is my life!

We can never give enough.
We are past all incidents.

By morning not even a sadness
not even a good-bye.

LOVE

Love, my love,
has shriveled and wrinkled to a habit.

It has grown too small for its clothes,
and spends its days staring
out at empty windows staring back.

Love is a memory; a legend
that has swallowed its creator.

It is a *memento mori*.

Love is a rabid wolf that roams
the forest of our nights
sinking its teeth into our lust.

Its poison slithers in our veins,
turning our hearts into urns for ashes.

Love, my love
is a sword, an arrow, a bullet
through the heart, every time
we open our lying mouths
to name it.

The exquisite corpses of love,
those promises of eternity
with their throats slit into wide smiles,
chests ripped open to expose what is missing,
litter the busy streets of betrayal.

Their open dead-eyes stare and see nothing,
not even the sky above them
raining blood my love.

WINTER MEDITATION

Everything is going at stone speed;
the playing of notes on my brain,
the music of music wafting through the rain
calling to the wolf.

A bell shimmers and shatters into crystal pieces
which glitter like snow beneath the gaze of lamplights.

Eyes look love in the eyes
and in less than a flicker of an eyelash
we've kissed years good-bye.

The years are sandpaper
going with, then against the grain;
rounding off the rough edges,
sanding raw the tender spots.

And what is an ancient truth
is revealed again in the howl of the wolf:

no matter how intertwined our lives get,
we live it and leave it
alone.

THE FIFTH SEASON
for E.F.

After the New Year,
before the Day of Atonement,
before we can be clean again,
we must visit with the dead.

The living gather at the cemetery gates
where charity rattles a can at us
asking for little, reminding us of a lot,
mumbles a thanks and lets us pass.

It is always colder in here.
The visible breath is a tap on the shoulder
of the old who hold onto the young;
the young shiver.

Along the path known by heart,
we walk toward the grave and notice
how, every year, our steps get slower.

In turn, each has their private moment
to murmur a prayer, say nothing
or wail at the heavens to ask what is to become of us.

Each puts a pebble on the headstone;
a tradition, a note to the living and the dead
to say we've been here.

Empty and feeling much better,
we turn to leave; promising more visits,
nicer flowers and a foot board next year.

Their memories wash us of the year's gathered pain.
This is the way the dead cleanse the living.
This is the way the dead keep on living.

This is the fifth season.

CAPTAIN POETRY
for bp

O silly Horseman
tongue galloping
twisting
soul kissing life
inhaling its breath
deep
exhaling its sounds
deep
in cacophonic cosmic giggles
in a country you made Dada

O bp!
Get up!
Get back on your horse!
On with the show!

This is not it!
This is not
it!

No!

So much more to do
new letters to sculpt out of air
new sounds to be
to be moved by
new pataphysical theories to test
in the ears of the deaf
days to make new
again and again and
a grain of sense to be gleaned from this world
nonsense to be

to be
bp

bp
this world
so silent without you

words weep
for their soul
for their mouth
for their bp
martyred
long before your time.

good-bye

  it's been brief but real

Rain Rain

Rain rain come again.
Rain rain
we've been wearing white too, too long,
wash this winter down the drain.
We want to change into a spring-green song.

Rain rain we itch and lust.
Rain rain
we yearn for your glistening shower,
and from beneath this winter's dirt and dust
we arch toward those clouds of passionate arousal.

Rain rain come right now.
Rain rain
slip your myriad of moist tongue tips
into every conceivable fold
and melt away this winter's icy hold.

Rain rain
rain right down to our roots,
where life begins again,
until our ecstasy rises through the shoots
and all is right as rain.

FLOWERS

Morning and spring and alive!

And just for those reasons
I thought of buying you flowers.

But good intentions and fine sunshine,
well, we know about them
and where they lead.

In the afternoon,
at the tip of the island lying on the grass,
under the spring sun,
I read a poem called Flowers;
all about death and decay.

After supper flowers came for you.

Made me wonder about good intentions
and how they are made good.

Our neighbours,
all dressed up on a day they shouldn't be,
were gathered like flowers.

With a smile you deliver the flowers
we assumed were for their special, happy occasion.

For years we have seen their youngest son
sitting on the verandah, chain smoking
in angry silence, fighting a private war,
finally losing, perhaps winning.

More relieved than sad at his successful suicide,
his parents are silent, stare into the evening.

It is springtime.

IMAGINE

Under stars
too many to imagine,
too far away to be more than just a flicker;
maybe no longer there,
there is life
asleep in rooms with lights on to keep the night away,
bodies in beds filled with fear.

We rummage for words to rub together
to start a fire, to keep warm;
for words that would be bright enough
to convince ourselves that days go by
for some important reason
and embrace
because of some revelation.

But every day we leave behind crumbs of failures;
lives done with.

Wearing the finest silks of murderers,
we are our own death squads.

We imagine
a world too hungry to imagine a heaven,
a world too real for hell.

HELLO

Hello!?
Anybody home?

Desperately inching toward a truth,
we have calculated our chances of being
and figured it as
n to the nth power;
less than winning the lottery.

We theorize Chaos,
Vacuum Genesis.

We know we happened.
We mutated to lucky,
evolved a language
sharper than claws,
deadlier than canines and
outgrew, outran, outwitted
all that hunted us.

We are now victims
of all that haunts us.

Our imagination knows no bounds.

In cranial laboratories,
wearing immaculate white coats,
we invent pleasure and torture
to be at our beck and call
and feed our too-human hunger.

This is a long distance call.

Someone, something about missing you:
a call about the living and the dying
who drop in unexpectedly
to remind us of what is paid
and what is still owed.

In every language,
we hurl sentimental and banal greetings into space;
desperately hoping to find someone, anyone,
to talk to about having evolved.

We leave behind
graffiti
shit
a trail of bleached bones.

The rest is silence.

REPORT ON THE 2ND HALF OF THE TWENTIETH CENTURY
Bk.8-11
KEN NORRIS

IN THE SPIRIT OF THE TIMES
KEN NORRIS

SILENCE
ELIAS LETELIER-RUZ
Tr. Ken Norris

SYMPHONY
ELIAS LETELIER-RUZ
Tr. Ken Norris

NA VRAITH ZVECER / AT THE DOOR AT EVENING
EDVARD KOCBECK
Tr. Tom Lozar
John Glassco Translation Prize Nominee

INTERIOR DESIGNS
ROBIN POTTER

HOW TO
ENDRE FARKAS
QSPELL Poetry Prize Nominee

THE OTHER LANGUAGE
ED. ENDRE FARKAS
Montreal Perfect Library Prize Nominee

DYING WITH AIDS / LIVING WITH AIDS
MARK LESLIE

THE COST OF LIVING
KENNER RADU
Governor General Award Nominee

THE MUSES' COMPANY

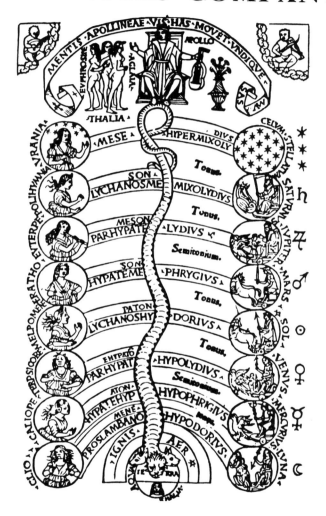

LA COMPAGNIE DES MUSES